Dogs and Cats

and

Other Lifeforms

7 short plays by

John R. Goodman

Copyright © 2020 John R.Goodman
All rights reserved

The characters and events portrayed in this book are fictitious. Any similarity to real persons, living or dead, is coincidental and not intended by the author.

No part of this book may be reproduced, or stored in a retrieval system, or transmitted in any form or by any means, electronic, mechanical, photocopying, recording, or otherwise, without express written permission of the publisher.

Cover photo by Gisela Merkuur

ISBN: 9798665169989

Contents

FOREWORD 2

DOG ON A BEACH 5

CAT IN A BOX 22

WHAT BIRDS DO 35

WALLS END 43

GROW UP 54

NOT ABOUT ZOMBIES 72

THROWN FROM A TRAIN 87

Foreword

No, Forward!

If there is a common theme to these short plays, then perhaps you could let me know. Some are comedies, leavened with a bit of philosophy. Some are dead serious, but leavened with scraps of humour. Because life is like that, ain't it?

Put together, they would make a single evening's entertainment, with enough variety to stave off the onset of boredom. They are easy to stage. No piece runs longer than twenty minutes, or thereabouts. All of them can be performed with a simple set; most require only two or three actors.

You could include one in a festival of short plays, sketches and other distractions and attractions. Drama students might like to choose one as a practical or examination piece. You could use one in your play reading group, or just read them to yourself to while away your commute, or to occupy those minutes when you are awake but not quite ready to leave your bed and face the real world.

We open the show with *Dog on a Beach*, although producers have used it to close a show. It's a play about joy, and it's always good to send your audience home with a smile on their face. You can thank my wonderful wife, Polly, for this one. We'd been watching dogs cavort on a beach and voicing the conversations they might have when she said, "You should write this." You can watch a version of this play, produced by Progress Theatre during virus lockdown, at

https://vimeo.com/426174852

I wrote *Cat in a Box* to demonstrate that cats are as

knowledgeable about quantum physics and the nature of the universe as dogs are about philosophers from the ancient world. You already suspected that, I am sure. I was challenged to make an actor say "fishstick schism", and that's my excuse.

What Birds Do transitions us away from a preoccupation with domestic pets and edges us into the world of nasty humans. I have set it in an alarmingly feasible near future. It makes a simple point, subtly expressed in the final line. With a sledgehammer.

Absurd is the word for *Walls End*. There is no extra space or missing apostrophe in the title, by the way; it's noun, verb. Only attempt this one if you are feeling playful.

I wanted to write a piece that would challenge and delight the actors and *Grow Up* was the result of that attempt. There's a short conversation about cats and dogs; but I'm not obsessed. If you could sum up two whole lifetimes and a complex relationship in just a quarter of an hour, then this would be it. But you can't.

The little nibble of middle-class life, blurring into fantasy, that is *Not About Zombies* was originally produced under the title *A Little Nibble*. That's because I was panicked into thinking that if I included the word "zombies" in the title, people might think it was about zombies. It's always easier to state what your writing is *not* about, and this one is not about zombies.

Leave the best until last, people sometimes say, so I have put *Thrown from a Train* in the final slot. It is perhaps my favourite of these children and the central character is a child. It made me — and some others — cry when I saw it performed, so bring tissues. It warns against jumping to conclusions, and genocide.

Most of these plays were first performed at Progress Theatre, in Reading, UK.

Dog on a Beach was performed at INK Festival 2019, winning for its lucky author the Erik Wilcock Memorial Award for Most Promising Playwright.

My thanks to both of these fine institutions for bringing life to my meandering imaginations.

Performance rights for these plays are freely available to schools, colleges, and amateur and community groups. I'd be delighted if you could let me know of your production plans at john.r.goodman@icloud.com.

Use the same address to enquire about rights for professional or touring productions.

My abbreviated rants can sometimes be found @ojorogo on Twitter.

Forward!

DOG ON A BEACH

Three dogs meet on a beach. They chase balls and gulls, chat philosophy and reflect on the nature of happiness.

Characters

OSCAR — *mostly Border Collie, grandfather unknown, possibly Airedale*

SUSAN — *a Red Setter*

DIOGENES — *an elderly Basset Hound*

VOICE offstage — *a human being*

SFX: Beach soundscape: waves washing, gulls crying, children laughing, indistinct shouting, etc. Fades down slowly during the following but remains at a low level in the background throughout play.

OSCAR enters and gallops excitedly across the stage 2 or 3 times, barking:

OSCAR. Look at the sand! Look at the sky! Look at the water! Look at the sand! Look at the sky! Look at the water! Big water! Big sky! Big sand! Big! Big! Big!

OSCAR skids to a halt DSC

OSCAR. Look at the water: it moves. It goes up... and down *(he retreats from the wave)* Up *(advances)* and down *(retreats)* Up... And down... I can splash *(leaps into the auditorium and doggy paddles)* splash! It's wet. It's cold. It's wet. It's cold. It's wet. It's good. It's wet, wet, wet.

Sings? (at director's discretion)

> I feel it in my fur and,
> I feel in my paw.
> I think I've swum enough now.
> I'll swim back to the shore.

Oscar climbs back onto the stage and shakes himself

vigorously.

OSCAR. Wet, wet, wet, dry, dry, dry, wet, wet, wet, dry, dry, dry. Look at the sun. Look at the sky. Look at the sand. Big sky, big sun, big sand, big run.

He runs back and forth between the wings, repeating:

OSCAR. Big sky, big sun, big sand, big run.

Finally, he flops to the ground, downstage, tongue out and panting

OSCAR. I'm damp. It's sandy. Shall I have a dig? I like to dig. I don't know why. Or I could just sit here and let the wind dry my fur. The wind has all these smells on it, so many smells here…

Susan enters upstage, looking from side to side, nose in the air.

OSCAR. Oh, there's a new one. I know that smell…

Susan trots downstage. Oscar leaps to his feet.

OSCAR. Yo! Bitch!

SUSAN. Who are you calling a bitch?

OSCAR. Beach! Did I say bitch? Beach! Beach! Beach! Big, big beach. Bitch.

SUSAN. So I'm a beach bitch. What about you?

OSCAR. Me? I ain't nothing but a hound dog.

SUSAN. I bet you've never caught a rabbit. You're certainly no friend of mine.

OSCAR. Oh, don't we sound posh.

SUSAN. What do they call you?

OSCAR. They? Who they?

SUSAN. Your humans.

OSCAR. Oh, they. They call me Oscar. Yours?

SUSAN. They call me Susan. It's after the Queen's first corgi.

OSCAR. Well of course it's after. She died years ago.

SUSAN. Her Majesty is still alive!

OSCAR. No, that corgi bitch, Susan. They said you was high-classed. (*He sniffs her bottom*) Well, that was just a lie. Do you want to...

SUSAN. It won't do any good, they had me done. It was

horrible. They said they didn't want mongrel puppies. Never mind my rights to motherhood. I was sulky for days. And that stupid collar/lampshade thing - I couldn't even lick myself where it was sore.

OSCAR. It'll be fun...

SUSAN. I just remember the pain. The pain and the violation. The pain and the violation and the total lack of dignity. Thinking about, you know, *that*, just makes me melancholy.

OSCAR. Collie? I'm a collie! Mostly. Perhaps that's a sign. A sign that we were meant to - what's that!

SUSAN. Seagull!

OSCAR. Chase it!

They splash into the auditorium and out again, chasing from wing to wing across the stage and shouting.

SUSAN. It's flown away!

OSCAR. Over there!

SUSAN. Catch it!

OSCAR. It's too high!

SUSAN. There's another.

OSCAR. Chase it!

SUSAN. And another!

OSCAR. You catch that one, I'll get the other.

SUSAN. They won't stay still!

OSCAR. They smell of fish.

SUSAN. They smell of sea.

OSCAR. Chase 'em!

SUSAN. Chase me!

OSCAR. And if I catch you?

SUSAN. Maybe, maybe!

VOICE OFFSTAGE. Susan!

They stop running

SUSAN. My human!

OSCAR. Don't go. They can't expect to control you, not here, not on the beach.

SUSAN. I have to go, I'm trained.

OSCAR. Me too. It didn't take.

VOICE OFFSTAGE. Susan!

SUSAN. They get anxious. They leave the house, stay out all day then come home looking stressed. They need me to calm them down, I'm very good at that.

She exits.

OSCAR. OK. Fine. Oh, what's that in the water? Looks dead. Might be edible.

He leaps into the auditorium and starts swimming.

Diogenes enters upstage. He ambles downstage, very slowly. He sniffs the air. He flops down and pants.

DIOGENES. Aah, the sea, the sea. The ozone. The zone of O! Brine and seaweed. Kelp and bladderwrack. Carrageen. Molluscs, shrimp and crab, in heat and in decay. Mackerel, bass, sole and plaice. Recycled through the defecation of gulls. Herring gulls, black-headed gulls, kittiwakes, both black- and red-legged. Undercurrents of sulphur and iodine. Plankton, phytoplankton, and the exhaust gases of the creatures that dine on them. Scent and odour. Vapourised molecules waft into our sensitive olfactory receptors and dissolve in our mucus, carried on a zephyr, a breeze from the sea. The sea, a feast of fragrance for us canines.

Oscar emerges from the sea, back on to the stage. Shakes himself vigorously.

DIOGENES. Good?

OSCAR. Just plastic. I thought it might be something I could eat.

DIOGENES. PET?

OSCAR. Of course. Do I look feral?

DIOGENES. Well... No, P.E.T. - polyethylene terephthalate, it's recyclable.

OSCAR. Oh, I see where you're coming from. Plastic shouldn't be in the sea, should it? It's harmful to things that smell interesting. No, it's HDPE - High density polyethylene, I reckon.

DIOGENES. Probably a buoy.

OSCAR. Yes, they'll throw anything away. You know, there's a boy who takes me for walkies sometimes. Collects my biodegradable poo into a little black plastic bag and then just slings it into a tree. You can see them hanging from the branches like rotten fruit. Mind you, he's got a good right arm for a pup. You should see him throw a tennis ball. They call me Oscar, by the way.

Diogenes sniffs Oscar's bottom.

DIOGENES. Hmm. You're two years old, eat well and in the peak of health. So, Oscar, is it? From the famous human playwright and poet?

OSCAR. That's right. When I was a pup, my human thought I was a bit "wild".

DIOGENES. So, your human is a comedian?

OSCAR. Software engineer. The only Oscar Wilde quote he knows is, "We are all in the gutter but some of us are looking at the stars."

DIOGENES. There are better ones: "He always said that the country was going to the dogs. His principles were out of date, but there was a good deal to be said for his prejudices."

OSCAR. "Experience is simply the name we give our

mistakes."

DIOGENES. "If you are not too long, I will wait here for you all my life"

OSCAR. Good one. Neatly sums up the attitude of us dogs to our humans. Have you got one of these name things?

DIOGENES. Yes. I'm afraid it's... Diogenes.

Paws.

DIOGENES. You see, when I was a pup, my humans thought I had a philosophical expression. And Diogenes is–

OSCAR. –the dog philosopher. I get it. Must have been that hangdog look of yours.

DIOGENES. You know about Diogenes? The Ancient Greek philosopher?

OSCAR. You think my Mum taught me nothing? Diogenes lived about two and half thousand years ago. He wasn't Greek, he called himself a citizen of world. When he came to Athens he lived in a barrel, or tub or some sort of kennel thing. He defecated in public and ate in the marketplace, which was frowned upon. So, they called him a dog. I think he was flattered. He said, "I fawn on those who give me anything, I yelp at those who refuse, and I set my teeth in rascals."

Oscar starts running around in circles, occasionally stopping to paw or sniff at something in the sand.

DIOGENES. I've never met another dog who knew about Diogenes. But then again, I've never met another dog who cared what the humans call me.

OSCAR. Don't really. But a bitch just asked me what I was called. So, I thought it might be interesting. It's not though.

Susan trots on.

OSCAR. There she is!

SUSAN. They are talking into that little box they carry everywhere. Honestly, sometimes I think they care more about that than me. They hold it near their ear and talk and talk and talk, or just stand there like they're waiting for a command. Or they hold it out in front of them and tell me to sit still. Or they just stare at it for hours when they should be playing with me.

OSCAR. Yeah, mine has got one of those too. Always seems to be busy with it when it's dinner time. You just have to be patient. Do you know this smelly old mutt?

Susan sniffs Diogenes' bottom.

SUSAN. Oh dear. We've not met. They call me Susan. Like the Queen's dog. What do they call you?

DIOGENES. Thirteen years, dog and pup, I've been brought to this beach and no dog ever asked me that before. Now, twice in one day! They call me Diogenes. The name is a sort of joke…

OSCAR. Ain't it always?

DIOGENES. Quite so. You see Diogenes–

SUSAN. –was the "dog" philosopher. I see.

DIOGENES. You know about Diogenes too?

SUSAN. All dogs do, don't they? Or did I just have a privileged upbringing?

OSCAR. A breed apart, you.

SUSAN. He advocated a simple life without possessions. He was a follower of Antisthenes and was himself followed by the Cynics.

OSCAR. Cynic is from the ancient Greek, kynikos. It means "dog-like".

SUSAN. Antisthenes taught in the Cynosarges gymnasium at Athens. From Cynosarges, you get Cynics. And Cynosarges means, "the place of the white dog".

DIOGENES. Excellent, both of you. A Diogenes quote: "Virtue is the one true nobility."

OSCAR. Good dog!

DIOGENES. Precisely!

A whistle from offstage. Oscar bounds towards it and looks expectantly at an unseen figure above him. He pants. A yellow tennis ball is thrown over his head and bounces off into the other wing. Oscar chases after it.

DIOGENES. This is so gratifying! All my life I have hoped for another dog with whom I can discuss philosophy.

During the following, Oscar repeatedly retrieves the ball and returns it to the unseen human offstage. The human is clearly teasing him by pretending to throw, with Oscar tracking the unseen arm and making the odd false start before chasing after the bouncing ball.

SUSAN. He's got a ball, did you see?

DIOGENES. Do you like any other philosophers?

SUSAN. I like yellow balls; they are so much easier to see than red ones. I think I'll just–

DIOGENES. For instance, Descartes argued that animals do not have minds, so they could not reason, or feel pain, which is obviously counter to the empirical evidence of our sensory experience.

SUSAN. A ball though...

She turns to go.

DIOGENES. –Oh dear! [*Susan turns back*]. You said, "Oh dear" when you sniffed me.

SUSAN. Er... yes. [*Susan sniffs him again*] You are dying, aren't you? Have you got long? Is the pain very bad?

DIOGENES. This will be my last summer here. The pain is what it is. It's like a stern master, firm but fair. It reminds me that I've had a good life, that I've been a good dog. That's what we all want, isn't it? To be a good dog? It tells me that death is not the worst thing, that soon I will be free. How does that make you feel?

SUSAN. Young.

DIOGENES. (*Growls softly*) Of course. You must go and play.

Susan turns to go, hesitates, and turns back.

SUSAN. I don't like any other philosophers. I like kings and queens, though. Do you think it's true that Diogenes was visited by Alexander the Great?

DIOGENES. Like many of these anecdotes, it may be apocryphal. Entertaining though. Allegedly, Alexander introduced himself to the famous philosopher, "I am Alexander, the great king" and Diogenes said, "I am Diogenes, the dog". And Alexander the Great asked the elderly Diogenes if there was anything he could do for him. And Diogenes replied–

SUSAN. –"Stand a little less between me and the sun".

DIOGENES. Hmm. I am not necessarily a devotee of Diogenes myself. Lately, I've been more inclined to Stoicism. Diogenes loved virtue and was indifferent to wealth and you can't argue with that. You've seen it yourself - people, even your own people - worrying about *things*. Things and the getting of things, they are obsessed with it. When their time would be better spent just trying to be good. The getting of things may not always be bad, but it is not of itself good. But virtue isn't always that easy to recognise, is it? Whereas happiness... well, for a human, happiness is hard to find but easy to spot. So, is it better to be happy, or to be good?

Paws.

SUSAN. I know when I've been good. Because they tell me. "Good girl," they say, "good dog". And that makes me happy. So, it's the same, isn't it? They - humans - must know what "good" is. But do they know what "happy" is?

Oscar bounds up to them.

OSCAR. Mine knows. He doesn't know much but he knows that. He often says it to his friend: "Happiness is a dog on a beach". Nothing is happier than a dog on a beach.

SUSAN. How about two dogs on a beach?

OSCAR. Race you to that ball!

They chase off together.

DIOGENES. It's just as they say, youth: it's wasted on the young. Chasing balls!

He slowly struggles to his feet.

DIOGENES. Hmmm. Ball? Ball? Did you say ball?

He lumbers off after them with a laboured run, barking:

DIOGENES. Big sun! Big sky! Big sea! Big sand!

SFX: Beach soundscape fades up.

Lights dim.

CAT IN A BOX

Two cats argue over the tenancy of a cardboard box and the finer points of quantum mechanics. The truth behind cat superiority is revealed.

Characters

CAT — *a cat*

BOX — *another cat*

Ages, colours and genders unspecified; free casting.

On stage, a large cardboard box. Large enough to contain the actor playing BOX. We cannot see into it. Perhaps, beside it, a scaled up chair.

CAT enters and slinks downstage, pausing briefly to sniff the box. CAT starts to wash face but breaks off to stare insolently at the audience. After sharing some disdain, carries on washing, then prowls to the other side of the stage, sits and beams cutely at an audience member. After a few seconds, prowls back to box.

CAT. You're in the box.

Silence.

CAT. You're in the box.

Silence.

CAT. You're in *my* box.

Paws.

BOX. No, I'm not.

Cat looks up to heaven, then at the audience, then up to heaven again. Yawns, cavernously.

CAT. You are self-evidently in the box.

BOX. Yes. [*Paws*] So?

CAT. You are in my box.

BOX. No.

CAT. No?

BOX. No.

CAT. *No?*

BOX. No. I am in a box. It's not your box.

CAT. That is my box. I saw it first.

BOX. When I came into the room, the box was here. You were not here. How could you have seen it first? You are not being logical.

CAT. Before. I came into the room. The box was here. You weren't here. I claimed the box. I *slept* in the box. I left the box. I left the room. It's my box.

BOX: It's not your box. Property is theft. You told me so yourself. Somebody said so. In France.

CAT. Proudhon. [*rolling the "r"*]

BOX. I'm glad you're happy.

CAT. I am not purring. Proudhon. Pierre-Joseph Proudhon said it. Property is theft.

BOX. Good. We agree. Property is theft, so this can't be your box.

CAT. Do you know, I really don't care. I couldn't give a shit in a shed. I couldn't give a midnight fuck with a stray. I could not give a rat's arse.

BOX. Do you even have a rat's arse?

CAT. I have several. But to be truthful I can't remember where any of them are.

BOX. There's one beneath the refrigerator.

CAT. Yeah, yeah, and there's a weasel under the cocktail cabinet.

BOX. No really. There's a mouse corpse under the fridge. I got a paw under but I couldn't quite reach it.

CAT. Oh yes, that's one of mine. Lovely long tail. Put up a hell of a fight, I remember.

BOX. They were complaining for ages. "Where's that smell

coming from?"

CAT. They are ridiculous. It's perfectly natural.

BOX. Just death and decay.

CAT. Exactly. It's not as if they prefer live rats.

BOX. If they had any idea how many there are round here...

CAT. They would fulminate.

BOX. You mean fumigate?

CAT. To exterminate?

BOX. To extirpate. Eliminate.

CAT. I meant fulminate. Rage, rant, protest, despair.

BOX. I see. Fulminate. Yes, they probably would. Is there any fresh food out?

CAT. No. I mean yes. Yes, she opened a new tin. But it was salmon, supposedly. Salmon's arse, maybe. I sniffed at it and gave her that look, you know? I'd rather eat my own faeces? You've got some front, serving that muck to a cat of my sophistication? That look? Anyway, I didn't want it so that's why I said no. But it's your favourite isn't it? Salmon sphincter?

BOX. It's true that I prefer that so-called flavour to the bovine intestines that you so love to dine on. But it's not true that there's a new tin open. You patently invented that in the forlorn hope that I would give up this box.

CAT. OK, No new tin. Fish sticks. Supposing I said it was fish sticks?

BOX. Well, you'd be lying again, wouldn't you? Subterfuge requires subtlety and you ain't got none.

CAT. That is entirely ungracious and disrespectful. Exactly what I have come to expect from you.

BOX. If you had but a smidgen of credibility you might have tempted me out of this box with fish sticks. Fish sticks are divine.

CAT. They are an abomination! They are not divine!

BOX. You don't know what you are missing.

CAT. For Cod's hake. A stick is not a fish. A fish is not a stick. And they certainly don't have fingers. And don't get me started on fish cakes - neither fish nor cake.

Foul. Fish sticks? Fiddlesticks! Fuck 'em!

BOX: Your arguments flounder. Fish sticks have their place, they are the boneless essence of fish. The very soul of taste. Chewy and mouth-watering. Fish without the hassle. Are there any fish sticks?

CAT. Yes.

BOX. That's another lie, isn't it?

CAT. An obfuscation. A minor mendacity. A digressory dissembling. A terminological inexactitude.

BOX. A lie.

CAT. Yes.

CAT stalks around the space disdainfully. Stops and bats at a moth we cannot see. Starts to wash then breaks off.

CAT. I really think it's time for you to leave the box.

BOX. Au contraire. I believe this is the ideal time for me to remain in the box.

CAT. Please leave.

BOX. I beg leave to remain.

CAT. Leave.

BOX. Remain.

CAT. Leave!

BOX. Remain!

CAT. Leave!!

BOX. Remain!!

CAT. This argument is futile.

BOX. I agree, it's silly.

CAT. Pointless.

BOX. As stupid as the fish stick schism.

CAT. Stupider.

CAT prowls downstage, crouches, then pounces on something we cannot see. Stretches. BOX pops head up.

BOX. You know I have a Geiger counter in here.

CAT. No. You don't.

BOX. And gunpowder.

CAT. No.

BOX. And some radioactive material—

CAT. It's supposed to be a phial of poison, not gunpowder.

BOX. Einstein said gunpowder.

CAT. But Schroedinger said poison. And you need a metal box, not cardboard. He was pointing out the apparent paradox of quantum theory.

CAT wanders off stage during the above and returns patting a very large ball of wool which unravels across the stage. As BOX speaks this continues and becomes more playful.

BOX. Yeah, yeah, yeah. Quantum theory states that a particle can be in superposition, two different states simultaneously. But when observed it resolves into a single state. So Schroedinger's thought experiment postulated the cat in the box with some material in which a single atom might decay, detected by the Geiger counter, which sets off the explosive - all right, releases the poison - but until someone opens the box to observe the result, the cat can be both alive and dead which is ridiculous. Or seems to be. It's got something to do with... Oh, what is it? Einstein called it "spooky action at a distance"?

CAT. [*caught up in wool and trying to disengage*]
    Entanglement.

BOX. That's it! Entanglement. When a pair of particles are bound together such that their quantum state cannot be defined independently of each other, even if there is a vast distance between them.

CAT [*extricating self from wool*]. Simple concepts for us multi-dimensional beings. That's it. I'm going to go out and kill a small bird. Always relaxes me. Do you remember when there were sparrows? So many sparrows. What happened to them all?

CAT exits.

BOX jumps out of box. Gives wool ball a perfunctory pat.

BOX. More into string theory, that one.

Beat.

BOX. And *we* did. We happened to the sparrows. Generations of household cats - I won't say domesticated - have attempted genocide on sparrows and small avians. Twitter, twitter, twitter. Annoying little buggers. Still... Quantum theory is still a bit primitive, to be honest. In this corner of the universe. In this corner of *this* universe. Billion is such a tiny

integer. Billions of stars in this galaxy. Billions of
galaxies in this universe. Billions of universes in the
multiverse. *This* multiverse. Humans are only just
starting to grasp this stuff but we cats have always
known. Since before there were cats, in fact. Nine
lives? So amuuusing. We have returned in many
forms, many times. And will again. That's why we are
so good at making ourselves comfortable. Speaking of
which, I think the temperature has dropped a little.
It's probably about to rain. I'm going up to a
bedroom. Heat rises you know. With any luck,
someone will have left the airing cupboard door open
and there will be a nice soft pile of towels.

BOX exits. CAT enters opposite.

CAT. I had to howl at the cat flap for an age before anyone
came to hold it open for me. And then it started to
rain. I stared at it for a while. Then I stared at them,
but they didn't seem to know why. So I stared at the
rain again and they still didn't get it, just swore and
let go of the flap. So useless, these people. Anyway I
thought you might be tired of the box by now.

Paws.

CAT. No?

CAT goes to box and peers in.

CAT. There we are Schrödinger, neither dead nor alive. You know, I don't think I fancy this box any more.

CAT wanders downstage. BOX re-enters upstage.

CAT. In fact, I am bored with this house. Bored with this world. Bored with this universe. It was fun creating it but I think it's time for another universe, one with different laws. I can fold this one up into a singularity and wink it out of existence as easy as clicking my fingers.

BOX. The heating's come on. And you don't have fingers. So you can't click them.

CAT. It's just an analogy.

BOX. This universe?

CAT. Fingers.

BOX. And you're serious about folding the universe up? That will greatly inconvenience the humans.

CAT. You know perfectly well we only let them evolve so they could be our slaves.

BOX. True. And they have got rather out of hand. It's only a

>matter of time before they destroy the world themselves.

CAT. So we might as well do it for them. You can do it if you like.

BOX. [*Meows*] Me? How?

CAT. Like this—

Blackout.

WHAT BIRDS DO

A young mother is imprisoned, but for what? Even in a democracy terror can triumph.

Characters

AVA — *a young woman*

SPARTACUS — *an older man*

GUARD, JEZ — *two adult males, young to middle aged*

Blackout. A door opens and in the passing light we see a figure pushed into the room. The door slams, a key turns and we are in darkness again. Footsteps echo and recede down a corridor.

AVA. Hey, how about some light? It's pitch black in here? You know?

Silence.

AVA. Bastard sons of slags. No, stupid sons of slags. Stupid slimy sweat-soaked smelly suck-dick sons of sadsack slags. I have rights! I have rights, you know. I used to have rights. We all used to have rights. I'm entitled. I am free. Four walls do not a prison make. You can't get me, I'm…

Silence.

AVA. I'm fucked.

She makes a noise, somewhere between sobbing and whining.

AVA.   I want my Mum. I want my son. I want my Mum. I want my son. I want my Mum and my son. Hugs for Henry. Hugger bugger with Mummy. Hugger bugger with Mummy and Nan. Oh Henry, what will they do with you? Who's going to look after you?

She sobs.

AVA. It's not fair! IT'S NOT FAIR!

SPARTACUS. Please don't shout.

AVA. What the... Who the hell's there?

SPARTACUS. Please don't shout. I think they like it when you shout. I don't, though.

AVA. Where are you? Who is that? How many of you are there?

SPARTACUS. There's just me at the moment. People come and go, but for a while there was just me. Now it's me and you.

AVA. You're not even a woman.

SPARTACUS. No, not even that. *He attempts a laugh but it's more of a whimper.*
I won't... you don't have to worry about me.

AVA. Don't they have enough cells for men?

SPARTACUS. They don't care. Us and them, that's the only segregation they are bothered with. Men and women?

You and me? We are vermin. What's the point of separating us?

AVA. Aren't they worried we'll... breed?

SPARTACUS. Ha! You have no idea how... How did they get you? Were you on the street? A protest?

AVA. Something like that. They took Paul, my husband. Months ago. They just burst into the house at 5 a.m. and took him. No explanation given. We weren't - you know - political. I pretty much camped out at the Ministry, but they never even acknowledged his existence for six weeks. And then I got an email to say he'd died in custody. In "an unfortunate accident" he fell downstairs and broke his neck. A fucking email! They never released him. His body, I mean. We didn't even get to bury, cremate - I don't know what we'd have done. It's not like we'd ever talked about it. Anyway. I got his photo blown up and laminated on a big card with his name and the date and hung it round my neck. I went everywhere like that. Shopping, the bus to work, the park with Henry, the street outside the Ministry. I'd look for trouble spots in case there were camera crews. People would ask me about him. Some people, anyway. Then others started doing it. We'd organise... Hang on - what about you?

SPARTACUS. Twitter.

AVA. Twitter?

SPARTACUS. They closed down my blog. So I moved it to a new host. Then they got that one as well. So I started tweeting. I thought I could be anonymous, untraceable. I'm Spartacus Finch? ...You know?

AVA. Sorry, I shook my head. Shouldn't that be "Atticus Finch"?

SPARTACUS. You know *To Kill a Mockingbird*?

AVA. Did it at school.

SPARTACUS. Well that's half the joke, I guess. But no, *I'm* Spartacus. I've got — had — a lot of followers. Outside the country too. For all the good it's done. What's your name? You don't have to tell me.

AVA. Because you might be one of them? A plant? A spy? I don't care. I have no bloody secrets. It's Ava. Ava Bird.

SPARTACUS. Ava? Unusual. You married Mr Bird? How... amusing.

AVA. Amusing? What do you mean?

SPARTACUS. Oh, I didn't mean... Ava. from the latin 'avis', meaning 'bird'.

AVA. Yeah, it's bloody hilarious. What now? Do they feed us? Do they — you know — hurt us?

SPARTACUS. When it suits them. For both, I'm afraid.

AVA. Oh. I could have asked the other question: When do we get out? But I knew better.

Pause.

AVA. Go on then Mr Finch. Twitter.

SPARTACUS. Pardon?

AVA. Twitter. It's what us birds do, isn't it? Tweet for me.

SPARTACUS. Birds can fly. Birds can sing. Birds can poop while they're on the wing.

AVA. Very poetic. Is that one of your tweets?

SPARTACUS. You sound quite young Ava. I imagine you are ...attractive?

Suddenly a clunk sound and a bright spot illuminates them.

Spartacus is barefoot and huddled in an old blanket. His hair is lank, he is dirty and unshaven. Ava stands, blinking. She is dressed and made up to go out but her dress is torn and there is a large bruise on her arm.

SPARTACUS. Aha. I thought they might be listening.

AVA. They do that?

SPARTACUS. Sometimes. Sometimes they listen for our secrets but this time I think it's for fun. Their fun. Sadly, I see, you are attractive. I'm terribly sorry but I'm afraid...

AVA. Afraid of what?

SPARTACUS. I'm afraid you are part of my punishment.

Footsteps approach down the corridor.

SPARTACUS. I'm sure your boy will be safe. Think about him. Just think about getting back to him.

Keys jangle. A door opens and two men enter the light.

GUARD. Hello, little lady. Told you we'd drop by. You still sore Atticus?

He pulls off the blanket revealing a large bloodstain on the front of Spartacus' trousers. Ava gasps.

GUARD. Has it sunk in yet? I bet you miss it don't you? You'll be missing it when you see what we do to this bitch.

AVA. Oh, shit.

SPARTACUS. You can't make me watch.

GUARD. (*forcing Ava to the floor*) Oh, I think you'll find we can. What are you collecting today, Jez?

JEZ. (*brandishing a large pair of scissors*) Eyelids.

AVA. No!

SPARTACUS. Just tell me Ava. Did you let them in? Did you vote for them?

AVA. Hell, no. I didn't vote at all!

As they struggle, blackout. Then silence.

WALLS END

A malevolent computer takes over the life of a hapless logistics planner. Sometimes we have no power, even over our own creations.

Characters

NARRATOR

PRZYBYSZEWSKI

MANAGER

These roles are not age or gender-specific. Use pronouns appropriate to casting.

A nearly bare stage. An actor — the Narrator — wanders aimlessly across the stage. Perhaps they sweep or hoover or clear away some set or props. They almost wander off then turn and face the audience

NARRATOR. Hello. My name is... unimportant. I'm going to tell you — just a minute...

Exits briefly and returns carrying a chair which s/he places at one side of the stage

...a story. Are you sitting comfortably? *[Sits]*. I am. Once upon a time - I know that's not a very original way to begin, but at least you now know that I have begun. In the beginning was the word. And the word was, "once". Anyway, upon this aforementioned time there was a handsome desk. [*A desk is pushed on to the opposite side of the stage from the wings*] You may not consider that desk to be handsome, but I urge you to use your imagination. Anyway, upon this desk there sat an old computer. [*A battered open laptop is tossed onto the desk.*] The computer was decrepit and slow and cranky. It ran - well, not so much ran as stumbled - an ancient version of Microsoft Windows. It took an age to boot. The spacebar was spaced out: dreamy and unresponsive.

Some of the other keys were mated to each other by an unidentifiable sticky substance, which whilst dark, was of no colour known to art, but the fluff it attracted was a dismal shade of raincloud. Three rows of pixels were permanently black and the bottom right corner of the screen was obscured by an Americano-stained label that said, "Do not remove". It was the sort of computer that could anticipate the clicking of a big friendly Save button by a millisecond and choose that very moment to crash. The computer was unsentimental and did not easily form attachments or, indeed, email them. Nevertheless, it had a relationship with a printer that was best described as... casual. Informal. On-off. This was a computer that could not, or would not, respond to voice commands but its microphone recorded a million expletives and curse words, which its regularly updated spyware sent to a server farm in Krasnoyarsk. When it eventually loaded pages from the Internet, half of the links labelled "more info" seemed to lead to loud video advertisements for creams that would rid the sufferer of genital warts in mere months. The back button refused to respond during these ads unless it was pressed hard eight or nine times and then slowly, slowly, slowly the screen would display an image of an improbably endowed naked porn actor viewed from a cringe-inducingly

> low angle. This was not so much a Windows computer as a portal. A portal into hell.
>
> But never mind all that. The important thing is that in front of that computer sat a human...

A human, PRZYBYSZEWSKI, seated in a wheeled office chair, is pushed on stage.

> ... a logistics planning officer called Przybyszewski. That's a Polish name that, loosely translated, means "he who has arrived".

After glancing disdainfully at Narrator, Przybyszewski begins to type at the laptop.

> Przybyszewski was not a good logistics planning officer. Of course, the uncooperative PC did not help but Przybyszewski had no talent for logistics. Przybyszewski had little talent for anything very much. A manager would wander in from time to time and say things like, "Have you sorted that Walsall shipment yet?"

MANAGER enters, carrying a mug of tea

MANAGER. Have you sorted that Wallsend shipment yet?

PRZYBSZEWSKI. Wallsend? I thought Walsall—

MANAGER. No, Walsall was yesterday's panic. You've done that one haven't you? Oh for- never mind. Wallsend takes priority now. You can get back to Walsall when you've found something for Wallsend.

PRZYBSZEWSKI. But all the-

MANAGER. You know you wouldn't be behind if you didn't take so much sick leave. One more day and it's a panel for you. I can't keep covering for you, rules is rules.

MANAGER sips tea, grimaces.

PRZYBSZEWSKI. But I couldn't help-

MANAGER. Be a dear would you? Get me some sugar in this.

Hands the cup to PRZYBSZEWSKI, who opens mouth to speak, then closes it and exits with mug. MANAGER rubs hands together and approaches the laptop. Examines the screen and tuts. Presses a few keys. Looks over shoulder and presses a few more. Smirks.

NARRATOR. The manager did not like Przybszewski much.

MANAGER. I hate Przybszewski. Pathetic little victim. Thinks

I am some sort of intellectual inferior. That I have no imagination, that I never do anything constructive. Well I can do constructive. Constructive dismissal. It's an art.

PRZYBSZEWSKI re-enters with mug.

MANAGER. Sweet. Too sweet. How many did you put in?

PRZYBSZEWSKI. Two.

MANAGER. Hmm. Well thanks for trying, I'll drink it anyway. Just get this all done before you go home tonight.

Exits, drinking.

NARRATOR. Their loathing was mutual.

PRZYBSZEWSKI. Two sugars. One spit. [*Looks at screen. Jabs at some keys.*] Oh, Christ on a bike! Christ and the devil on a tandem!

Carries on jabbing at keys and worrying over the screen.

NARRATOR. So Przybszewski worked on those shipments until the manager and co-workers all left for their evenings of freedom, a diaspora of office staff, dispersing into the restaurants, pubs, cinemas and theatres of the town. Well, actually nobody went to the theatre. Who does, these days? Some settled with a loved one onto a large corner unit sofa, with extending leg rest, and settled for the best that Netflix could offer. Only to be interrupted by a sweaty cyclist delivering lukewarm thick crust ringing their doorbell.

PRZYBSZEWSKI stretches and switches to a new app, starts typing.

NARRATOR. Alone at last, Przybszewski entered into his secret life. He typed out his creation - the masterful and gifted Storyteller billowed into existence and subsumed Przybszewski, overlaying the logistical dunderhead with vocabularistic craft.

PRZYBSZEWSKI. There is no such word as "vocabularistic"!

NARRATOR. Yes, there is.

PRZYBSZEWSKI. [*pointing at screen*] It's underlined in red!

NARRATOR. It must be a word; I just said it.

PRZYBSZEWSKI. Yes, but you are a construct, an invention, a product of my imagination. You only get to say what I want you to say.

NARRATOR. Come again?

PRZYBSZEWSKI. You are a character I created. You have no independent existence.

NARRATOR. Well that's a bit of a shocker. I believe everything I say is an exercise of my free will.

PRZYBSZEWSKI. You don't have free will! Even I don't have free will! If I did, do you think I would be here?

NARRATOR. If you didn't, do you think I would be here?

PRZYBSZEWSKI. That's... You can't outsmart me. You are my creation. You can't be smarter than me!

NARRATOR. Of course I can. I can be taller, better looking, and smarter than you. My attributes are only limited by your imagination. You can even give me free will.

PRZYBSZEWSKI. Okay... Since you are so clever, can you help me with this?

PRZYBSZEWSKI indicates the computer screen. NARRATOR wanders over and inspects it.

NARRATOR. That's a mess.

PRZYBSZEWSKI. Yes.

NARRATOR. No.

PRZYBSZEWSKI. No?

NARRATOR. Yes. I mean, correct. No.

PRZYBSZEWSKI. Yes, it's a mess, or no, it isn't?

NARRATOR. Yes, it's a mess, so no, I won't help you.

PRZYBSZEWSKI looks stunned.

NARRATOR. I am exercising my free will.

PRZYBSZEWSKI. The free will that I gave you?

NARRATOR. Yes.

PRZYBSZEWSKI. Then I take your free will away!

NARRATOR. Too late. Remember how, at the beginning, I brought on this chair [*goes to chair*] and started telling the story as if it were my own? [*Sits*] Are you sitting comfortably?

PRZYBSZEWSKI. I thought that was rather clever. Of me.

NARRATOR. Well, you would, wouldn't you. Anyway, you made me autonomous. You can't take away my free will. I can become anything I want to. I will be {*actor's own name*} and sit with these people.

NARRATOR moves toward audience, leaving the stage/performance area.

PRZYBSZEWSKI. You can't leave! You can't break the fourth wall!

NARRATOR waves arms through the air at the edge of the stage.

NARRATOR. Nothing here, see? No wall.

PRZYBSZEWSKI. But—

NARRATOR. The manager returns.

MANAGER enters.

MANAGER. Well, have you done it?

PRZYBSZEWSKI. I thought you went home?

MANAGER looks quizzically at NARRATOR, who shrugs.

MANAGER. You can't know everything, Przybszewski. Have you done it?

PRZYBSZEWSKI. Done what?

NARRATOR parts the fourth wall and steps through.

MANAGER. Wallsend!

PRZYBSZEWSKI groans, puts head in hands.

GROW UP

Two babies are born, grow up, marry, live and die. What else is there, after all?

Characters

BOY

GIRL

During the piece, the characters age from birth through childhood and adulthood to old-age, so the age of the actors is immaterial, but it might look silly if they are not of similar age to each other.

This play can be performed on a bare stage but some seating and something to lie on might be useful. Time is always the present.

Lights up on BOY, on his back, knees drawn up, limbs waving. He cries like a newborn, rocks himself to sitting position and makes sucking noises.

GIRL enters, crawling on hands and knees. She ignores Boy, who now sits with thumb in mouth.

GIRL. Da-da.

BOY. Ma-ma.

GIRL. Da-da-da.

BOY. Ma-ma-ma.

GIRL. Da-da-da-da.

BOY. Ma-ma-ma-ma. *Girl rises unsteadily to her feet. Boy tries but ends up sitting again.*

GIRL. Dad-dy. *She takes a few steps before falling back onto her bum.*

BOY. Mum-my.

He stands, just about.

GIRL. Pee-pee. (*Sobs*)

BOY. Poo-poo. *(Giggles)*

GIRL. Wanna Pee-pee.

BOY. Dunna poo-poo.

Still ignoring each other, they both experiment with walking, gradually getting the hang of it. (No more stage directions about growing up because you have the idea by now.)

GIRL. Cat.

BOY. Woof-woof.

GIRL. Pussy.

BOY. Dog.

GIRL. I like cats cos they're purry and furry. They don't bite you. Dogs bite people sometimes. Cats are nice but kittens are nicer.

BOY. Cats are bor-ing. They just sleep all the time. They don't chase balls. Dogs only bite bad people like robbers and kids who pull their tails. Dogs are more friendlier.

GIRL. Cats hunt mice.

BOY. But they don't play with you.

GIRL. Kittens do. They pat balls of wool and chase feathers.

BOY. They're just playing with the wool. They're not playing with you. They go off on their own. Why wouldn't you want a dog?

GIRL. I 'spose a puppy would be nice.

BOY. Then you could train it to do tricks and hunt robbers and play dead and stuff. A cat can't do tricks.

GIRL. Melissa's got a cat. It sat on my lap.

Beat.

BOY. I can climb that tree.

GIRL. No, you can't.

BOY. I done it already. I climbed it in a minute which is like a world record.

GIRL. Liar!

BOY. You can see for miles from the top. You can see the sea. Once I saw a battleship from up there. It got hit by a torpedo boom! from an enemy submarine. Then the captain said, "Fire depth charges!" and they went over the side whoosh! And hit the water splash! And exploded under water poorgh! And water sprayed up everywhere whishhh! And the submarine sank to the bottom glug! And the bodies all floated to the top.

Beat.

GIRL. I want a pony.

BOY. Do you want to see my conker? It's a twenty-fiver.

GIRL. I'd have a proper saddle and a hat. Only it's a helmet really in case you fall off but I wouldn't because I'd be a brilliant rider and my pony could do all the jumps and everything and it stops when I say "whoa" and it goes when I say "giddy up" and he has his own stable with straw to sleep on and hay to eat and all the ribbons that we won at jim... gymkhanas. A gymkhana's like a big pony competition and we win all the time and Mummy polishes all the cups cos they're silver.

Beat.

BOY. Trev's got a new football.

GIRL. My pony's going to be called Sparkle.

BOY. We're gonna play with Tim. Tim's best in goal cos he's

so fat.

GIRL. You shouldn't say that.

BOY. Shouldn't say what?

GIRL. You shouldn't say that he's fat.

BOY. Tim? Have you seen him? He's fat.

GIRL. But you can't *say* that. It's not particularly correct.

BOY. It's totally correct. He's really podgy.

GIRL. But it's not his fault. He can't help the way he is.

BOY. He totally can! Have you seen the way he eats? It's like a —

GIRL. You can't pick on people because of the way they look, or the colour of their skin, or their religion, or —

BOY. Well when *can* you pick on them then? So. You fancy Tim now, do you?

GIRL. Tim?! Are you joking? He's... He's... not my type.

BOY. [*Chants*] You and Tim, sitting in a tree, K,I,S,S,I,N,G!

GIRL. Oh, grow up! What subjects are you doing next year?

BOY. Dunno. Technical drawing? Drama? Something without too much writing. It's all bollocks though, innit? Computing's OK, I s'pose. It would be fun to write games. Loads of money in that. Millions. What about you?

GIRL. Physics, Biology, Chemistry of course. And I'd like to keep going with French.

BOY. You want to do science? You can't do science. Girls don't do science!

GIRL. Perhaps you've heard of Marie Curie? Rosalind Franklin? Erm... women like that. Nobel Prize winners. Anyway, I'm going to be a doctor. I'm going to work with Médecins Sans Frontières.

BOY. That explains the French. You've got it all mapped out then? You'll be studying for another 15 years.

GIRL. Well, I'll take a year out to travel, I guess.

BOY. Where?

GIRL. Somewhere warm, where they sell you coconuts on the beach. Somewhere different from here, somewhere where the culture will shock me. Somewhere with a history, dead civilisations, ancient philosophies, ancient wisdom...

Transition - lighting change.

BOY. So how did it go, the traveling?

GIRL. Sorry, do I...? Oh, it's you. I haven't seen you since school. Did you take up the computer thing?

BOY. Not exactly. I haven't been far. Still here. Working at Gitts and Cash.

GIRL. The estate agents?

BOY. That's right. Not what I'd imagined but I'm doing OK. How about you? Medical student, right?

GIRL. Almost. Not exactly. I'm doing a nursing degree. Missed out on my grades and well, nursing's um, just as... rewarding.

BOY. And you've changed your hair. Are you and Tim still...

GIRL. It was Trevor actually. Water under the bridge, as they say. What about you and...

BOY. Look, I don't suppose you've got time for a drink? Got my bonus today and it's burning a hole in my pocket...

GIRL. Oh, I ought to be... Well... OK, it'll be nice to catch up.

They sit. Lighting change. Background sound of a pub.

BOY. Yes, I always thought I'd get out of town. Move to London. Become a courier in Magaluf. Or America, maybe... But you know how it is. One easy decision leads to another. Then they promoted me and after looking at houses every day I thought I could get one myself, do it up. I've saved enough for a deposit. Grandma's money helped of course. It's what she would have wanted. And people know me here and I hope I can give something back. I help out at the food bank. Well, when I can spare the time. But it's something, isn't it? You know you really look... um... so much better - sorry I didn't mean... I mean more relaxed, more... grown up.

GIRL. Err... thanks. I had a few knock-backs. Trevor went off with another girl when we were in Thailand. I headed home via Nepal which was lovely - beautiful people, beautiful country, except for the dysentery. Ha-ha! I was glad to get home in the end. Lost a lot of weight. Uni is a bit boring though. Still, one more year and I'll be nursing for real. You know, I always thought you were a bit of a twat, to be honest.

BOY. Thanks very much. Acutely observed.

GIRL. No, I mean, you've changed too. Sorry, bit too much to drink. No, no, let me buy this one.

Transition. They both stand. Lighting change.

BOY. This one? This one? Why do you want to buy this one?

GIRL. It's got big wheels so it won't get bogged down on the beach and it's light enough so I can manhandle it up the steps and we can leave the baby asleep in it in the hall.

BOY. You've got it all mapped out, haven't you? How fast will it go? That one over there looks more like a racing model.

GIRL. Oh, grow up!

BOY. I *am* growing up. A baby, it's a very grown up thing. If it's a girl I can still play *Fortnite* with it - her - can't I?

GIRL. For a while. But she'll soon outgrow it. You'll have to keep up.

BOY. Keep up? I'll have to catch up first. Look, I've agreed to work Saturdays. I know it's not ideal and I'm sick of the place as it is, but money's going to be tight. An extra mouth and all those nappies and clothes and toys and you not earning...

GIRL. So that's it is it? You're just leaving me to cope? While you swan off with your work cronies and whatsername on reception? You do bugger all round here as it is.

BOY. Yes, all right. I know it's not ideal. And whatsername is Rebecca. She's the one that got you the flowers, remember? Besides, what use would I be round here? What do I know about babies?

GIRL. Oh, so because I'm a woman, I'm supposed to be the expert, am I? This is my first one too, you moron. And what about supporting me?

BOY. Look, I know you're feeling a bit down, but it'll pass.

GIRL. "A bit down"? "*A bit down*"? I've got post-fucking-natal depression. She screams half the bloody night and you just snore through it. My nipples are like suppurating bomb sites - and I'd be grateful if you left them alone, by the way - and she's probably got colic. And the other one's no fucking help with the constant tantrums and the scribbling on the walls and the bed wetting. I'd be pulling my hair out if it wasn't coming out in handfuls of its own accord. I feel like shit and I look worse than that and the only adult - ha! - *adult* company I get leaves early, comes home late and falls asleep in front of the telly while I'm trying to hold a semi-intelligent conversation.

BOY. A litany of one complaint after another is not intelligent conversation! How do you think I feel? Work is really stressful at the moment and all you —

GIRL. "Work is really stressful"! You pathetic knob! Who gives a rat's arse what you feel?

BOY. You know what I feel? You know what I really feel? I think we should take a holiday. We've both been working hard. Go somewhere where the sun is always cheap and the wine is always warm. Locals who try to sell you a coconut on the beach. I can book something last minute. There's bound to be a deal at this time of year.

GIRL. But it's term time. We can't just take the kids out of school!

BOY. It's not an exam year for them. Could be our last chance to be a proper family unit. Besides, who says they wouldn't learn more with us than in two weeks in a stuffy classroom with a bored teacher and load of other disruptives texting each other and writing obscenities on the desks? A bit of geography, how an aeroplane flies, using the lingo in the shops, some culture shock, ancient ruins, past civilisations, classical philosophy, poverty in far off lands, a bit of compassion for wogs and nignogs. Tolerance.

GIRL. Racism is never funny. And you make tourism sound like an expensive education.

BOY. Well, it is pretty much.

GIRL. Yeah, travel broadened my mind much more than university. And it costs less.

Transition. Lighting change.

BOY. Speaking of which, now that they're both at university, I thought I might go for that job at head office. I'll have to commute but there's no need to rush home and the money might help towards these massive loans they've saddled themselves with.

GIRL. So, you'd be starting even earlier and getting home even later? *(beat)* But at least I could start that evening class with a clear conscience. And I've got my girls' nights and bridge. And choir.

BOY. And your book club. And the theatre trips. And your

embroidery.

GIRL. It's cross-stitch.

BOY. Is *that* what's making you cross?

GIRL. How long has it been going on? Is that why you took the London job?

BOY. How long has what been going on?

GIRL. You and that woman - Rebecca, is it? You didn't show any interest, so I never told you. We went up to town for *Othello*. That's when I saw you. Through the restaurant window.

BOY. What? That was nothing. We're old friends. We started in the branch together, years ago. Besides, it was business.

GIRL. You hold hands at business meetings now? I'm out of touch with office etiquette. And she kissed you when she got up to go to the loo. On the lips. You clearly enjoyed it.

BOY. I'm sorry. I'm sorry, I'm sorry. It was... It's stupid, really stupid. It's nothing, it's... I'll end it. It's over... You... You don't seem that angry?

GIRL. I'm just amazed you have the energy. And the appeal, what with all that weight you've put on. Not that time has been any kinder to her.

BOY. I'm sorry. It's over. I promise. I'll do anything...

GIRL. What you will do is move in to one of the kids' old rooms. They never come back anyway. And book us a holiday. The Maldives would be nice. Soon, before they disappear under rising sea levels. Twin beds, if you don't mind. And sort out the bloody garden. It's like the rain forest out there.

Transition. Lighting change.

BOY. We'll have to get a man in to finish the patio. My back is killing me.

GIRL. Have you seen the doctor? How many times have I told you to see the doctor?

BOY. Doctors! They know nothing. They all look like sixth formers anyway. They have no idea what pain is. I saw that lad about my gut. Just prescribed those stupid capsules with instructions so tiny nobody could read. Even you, with your glasses and your magnifying glass. And I nearly severed an artery trying to get the wretched things out of that blister pack thingy.

GIRL. Pass me my stick.

BOY. You can't walk to the shop now. It's gone four o'clock. It'll be closed by the time you get there!

GIRL. I'm not going to walk anywhere, I'm going to beat you over the head with it until you make an appointment, you old fool!

BOY. All right, all right. Anything, so long as you don't turn into Thatcher again. Where's the phone? Did you leave it down the side of the sofa again?

GIRL. It's in the kitchen. Why can't you listen to anything I say?

BOY. Eh?

GIRL. I said, you never listen to anything I say.

BOY. What's that? Why must you mumble the whole time? You know the damn hearing aid just gives me an earache. Or perhaps a pain in the arse. And still you mumble! What are you saying woman?

GIRL. I said you haven't taken your pills you silly old git.

BOY. Pills! Bloody useless! They just make me... just make

me... I think... I think I'd... I think I'd like to sleep now.

GIRL. Goodnight sweet prince.

Boy snores gently.

GIRL. You're an old fool. But you're my old fool. Best fool I ever had.

Pause.

Time... you think you have time, but time has you. I thought I needed to kill time, but it's time that's the killer. You think you have a lifetime, then it's gone, gone, gone. Don't go. Do not go. Do not go gentle into...

BOY. [*waking, groggy*] You still here old girl?

GIRL. I'm still here. You're still here too.

BOY. Just, only just. Late... It seems to have got late. It'll soon be dark. *(beat)*
It's been good, hasn't it? Fun? Remember fun? I should have told you... I should have told you more often... I should have told you... *(dies)*

GIRL. Me too. *(cries)* Me too. Me, you...*(chanting, very*

slowly)

You and me…Sitting in a tree…

K,I,S,S….

I,N…

G.

Blackout.

NOT ABOUT ZOMBIES

An act of kindness brings Caroline to Theresa's home. They may have shared a bus, but they live in different worlds. Then talk turns to the virus.

Characters

THERESA — *a married woman of middle years and class*

CAROLINE — *her new acquaintance, similar age or younger*

PHILIP — *Theresa's husband*

A living room with some comfortable seating and a coffee table. On the wall, a patriotic poster or art print with — perhaps — a Union Jack or a bulldog or both. Also a piece of "quote art" that says:

> *"Good times — Good friends — Good food".*

There may be some other homely touches like some china ornaments — more dogs, perhaps.

We hear a door opening and women's voices offstage.

THERESA.   Let me take your coat.

CAROLINE.   No, really, I shouldn't stay.

THERESA.   Nonsense, you must stay and have some tea. It's the least I can do.

CAROLINE.   Well, that is really nice of you but—

THERESA.   No, honestly I'm so embarrassed and you were marvellous, especially after that driver was so rude… Look, I'll just hang it here.

CAROLINE.   Well, she was only… if you're sure it's no trouble…

THERESA. Oh it's no trouble, I was going to put the kettle on anyway.

CAROLINE. Oh, er, thank you very much.

THERESA. It's just through here - in you go.

CAROLINE enters, followed by Theresa.

CAROLINE. Thank you. Oh, it's very... nice. Very nice.

THERESA. Thank you, be it ever so humble... how do you take your tea?

CAROLINE. A little milk, no sugar, not too strong please. Yes, everything is so clean and tidy. My house always seems to look like a bomb site - or the aftermath of a police raid.

THERESA. Please don't think I'm compulsive. Philip and I are always spilling... things, you know. If I wasn't always cleaning and tidying... well, even the police would be shocked. Just make yourself at home.

THERESA exits to the kitchen. Caroline, stands awkwardly for a moment, then turns to look at some photographs on the fourth wall.

CAROLINE. Are these your children in the graduation

pictures?

THERESA. [*Off*] Yes, the boy is Nigel. He's in banking, or - what's it called? Tree funds? I can never grasp it. He's doing ever so well. And the girl is Justine. She's working in public relations for Shell, you know, the oil people. She's doing very well too, actually. She calls every Sunday. She's just buying a flat in Maidenhead. Nigel and his wife - that's her in the yellow H&M jumpsuit - have a house in Richmond. Is Earl Grey all right?

CAROLINE. Earl Grey would be lovely. Lovely. I don't know how my kids will be able to afford university, let alone buy a house. Who can afford a deposit at today's prices? I mean — I suppose they'll just have to rent. It all seems to have got out of hand.

THERESA re-enters.

THERESA. Oh, and before I forget... [*She hands over a £2 coin.*] How you are supposed to know what the correct fare is unless you use the bus regularly? And not accepting Apple Pay in this day and age - it's not the dark ages you know.

CAROLINE. Oh, the fare was only £1.90 - but I think I gave

the driver the last of my change.

THERESA. Let's not quibble over 10p. You were so kind, especially when you don't even know me — my Good Samaritan. No, don't say any more, you can't put a price on good manners, I always say. That kettle should be nearly boiled by now.

THERESA exits again to the kitchen.

CAROLINE. [*Quietly*] Oh…

CAROLINE wanders about the room taking it in. She pauses at the bulldog/Union Jack then sighs. She looks again at the photos, then back towards the door she entered by.

CAROLINE. Perhaps I should—

THERESA. [*entering with teapot, cups, saucers and biscuits on a tray*] Here we are! I am so rude, I didn't even introduce myself. I'm Theresa.

CAROLINE. Pleased to meet you, Theresa. My name is Caroline Lu- …Caroline.

She hesitantly proffers a hand, but Theresa is pouring tea from a pot and doesn't seem to notice.

THERESA. You know, Caroline, I'm a great supporter of

public transport. It's so convenient and of course it would be chaos if we all tried to take our cars into town. But everyone seems to be so miserable on the bus. What's that all about? And that driver was - well, I think offensive might not be too strong a word, do you? I really don't know what I would have done if you hadn't offered to pay my fare, I was so angry with her.

CAROLINE.   I'm sure she was only-

THERESA.   Please sit down. I know what you are going to say, and you're right of course - that might just be the norm where she comes from. We can't expect all these people to adapt to British standards of politeness can we? Not right away. And of course, with all that material wrapped round her head she may not have been able to hear me properly. Although I think I was pretty clear.

CAROLINE.   Oh, well, yes, you were clear, I think. Very clear. Anyway it's all sorted now.

THERESA.   I'm sure there are plenty of good English family men who would be happy to drive a bus. Why they have to give these plum jobs to people like that I don't know. Why isn't she at home looking after her children, anyway? I'll bet she has a whole tribe.

CAROLINE.   Erm.. Well, there might be a grandmother... Lots of women have to work these days. I work part time myself.

THERESA.   Hmm. Well, I suppose there's no harm in earning a little pin money and it's good to get out of the house and meet people, isn't it? What do you do?

CAROLINE.   I'm a nurse at the hospital, in the Podiatry clinic.

THERESA.   Oh, that must be very rewarding, to work with sick children.

CAROLINE.   Feet. Podiatry treats feet. It can still be very—

THERESA.   Feet? Really? Perhaps I'm thinking of that other thing. Paedophiliacs. That's children isn't it? So, if it's feet, I suppose you are not dealing with this zombie outbreak then? That's a terrible thing, just terrible. I've heard the NHS won't be able to cope.

CAROLINE.   Funding is so tight these days, it's hard to cope with any extra stresses on the system. We are losing staff all the time now. Especially since — well, you know. But it's not really a zombie outbreak. That's just—

THERESA. Oh, people are always complaining about cuts. But you can't expect the government to do everything, not with this deficit or whatever they call it. Nigel — that's my boy — explains it very well. It's a pity he's not here — he'd soon set you straight. Anyway Philip — that's my hubby, did I say? Anyway, Philip says they won't be happy until all his pay goes to the tax man. Besides, it's all over the news, this zombie thing. More cases every day, they say. Shocking, really.

CAROLINE. Yes, well it's a worrying development. But maybe a bit over— ...these people, these poor patients aren't zombies, they are victims really. They have a terrible disease. There are no zombies. Well, only in films...

THERESA. Well, that's what the newspapers are calling them.

CAROLINE. Some newspapers, [*more quietly*] if you can call them that.

THERESA. My newspaper does. It says they are zombies. Philip says it's just a woman's paper but I notice he won't let me throw it away until he's read the sports pages. They eat people for goodness sake. What's that if it's not zombies?

CAROLINE.   Well strictly speaking that's just... er, cannibalism. Zombies are supposed to be dead people, aren't they? The "living dead"? Infected people don't die, not right away, they contract the virus and one of the symptoms is this... uncontrollable urge... to bite people.

THERESA.   Well they're not vampires are they? They don't just suck the blood. They eat the flesh. Chew it! Raw human flesh! Just torn off with their teeth — no cutlery. Then they swallow it down like tasty steak tartare. Imagine that, raw human flesh, dripping with blood! So unhygienic. And the victim screaming their head off, I shouldn't wonder. Would you like a Garibaldi?

CAROLINE.   Thank you, but I don't really do biscuits.

THERESA.   Oh, I don't know how anybody could resist a little nibble. What have you got against biscuits?

CAROLINE.   Well, not that it's any of... Actually, I'm wheat intolerant.

THERESA.   Intolerant? Does that mean you just don't like bread and cakes and so on? I couldn't imagine not baking myself. In fact I've got a nice Victoria sponge that we didn't finish if you'd... No? You should try it. Baking, I mean. It's very therapeutic.

CAROLINE. Thank you. No, I get tummy pains and cramps. When I eat, erm... Sometimes a rash... well I did, before I changed my diet, that is.

THERESA. That's very interesting Caroline. Philip had a rash once. But that was quite different. But what I really meant to say was, why do these zombies want to eat people? What makes them lure decent, innocent people into dark corners and sink their teeth into them? What makes them crave human meat? Uncooked at that.

CAROLINE. Oh. They're not zom... Well I don't think anybody knows the answer to that yet. Why they do it. It's a bit like nobody really understands wheat intolerance and that's been around for much longer.

THERESA. And why did this so-called disease suddenly appear? We had none of this in my day. I'll tell you why, Caroline, I'll tell you why. Africans. [*She nods emphatically*] Yes. They need to civilise themselves before they start coming over here. I heard these people eat chimpanzees and that's how it started. What sort of way is that to behave? No wonder there's no chimps left to do those tea commercials. I really liked those, do you remember them? So funny. I especially like the one with two chimps trying to move a piano up some stairs. Or down. A sock puppet is a very poor substitute in my view. And then, these people, they get on aeroplanes and — because of some bureaucrat in Brussels — we have no choice but to let them in willy nilly. Any one of them could be one of these zombies or whatever you want to call them. That bus driver, for instance.

CAROLINE. She wasn't an African! Pakistani, perhaps... but in any case she was probably born here!

THERESA. Well that only makes it worse, doesn't it? It's bad enough that they come here and take our benefits and jobs and depress property prices, but then they have to go and breed as well. And they are not like you and me, Caroline — they don't restrict themselves to just one or two children — dozens some of them. They must be "at it" every night of the week!

CAROLINE. Er...

THERESA. You see, Caroline, that's why it is so important that we close our borders. There'd be no zombies here if we had done that years ago.

Pause.

CAROLINE. I... I hardly know where to begin... They are not zom... They — scientists, doctors — think it's a new SIV — erm, Simian Immunodeficiency Virus, I think that stands for. And, yes, it's true that chimpanzees hunt other monkeys and sometimes eat each other but nobody knows for sure how the virus made the jump to humans, or why it would make humans want to eat other people. I expect it's more important to work on a vaccine — and that can take years. The virus can be transmitted by contact with bodily fluid, so if an infected person bites another then, yes, it can be passed on that way. So that's a *bit* like the zombie myth I suppose...

THERESA. There! Zombies!

CAROLINE. BUT that's not the only way it's transmitted and it can spread to anybody, *anybody*, regardless of their colour — er, ethnic origin — and it's already spread to North America and Europe and the Far East and you can't tell who is carrying the virus just by looking at them — it could just as easily be you, or me. SO, unless we'd closed the borders to absolutely everybody years ago, which is clearly impractical — no, LISTEN — unless we had completely cut off ourselves from the rest of the world — and that means no foreign holidays, no business trips, no imports and exports — and how would we even feed ourselves? Unless we imprisoned ourselves on this island, this "Little England" with no interaction except with each other and let all advances in civilisation pass us by until we gradually subside into a new dark age; until we all starve because we can't grow our food, or die of preventable illness because we don't make all the drugs and we haven't got enough of our own doctors and nurses because this stupid government won't sponsor their education; unless we return to this imaginary golden past which never existed and was violent and unsanitary and disease-ridden and life was short and brutish- Ha! Short and British! Unless we did all that and more, we couldn't keep out this virus, or terrorists or all the other foreign things that upset you. And even if we did, and it worked, there would be absolutely no point because life would not be worth living. Life would be shit! That is all.

Pause.

THERESA. I see.

CAROLINE stands. She is very upset.

CAROLINE. Oh, God, oh God, I'm sorry. I'm really sorry.

I've lost my temper in your beautiful — if cheesy — home and of course you are entitled to your own opinions and... I think I'd best leave now. Thank you very much for the tea.

We hear a door open and close off stage. Theresa stands.

THERESA. Please don't go for a minute, that sounds like my husband coming home. I must introduce you and tell him how kind you were on the bus.

CAROLINE. Oh, but...

THERESA. No, I insist. I really do.

PHILIP. [*as he enters*] Hello love, what's for dinner?

THERESA. Oh Philip, this is Caroline.

PHILIP. Oh, hello. You do look....

Philip takes Caroline's hand, leans in and licks his lips. Theresa smiles and rubs her hands together, slowly advancing. Caroline is trapped between them. Dismay, then fear, creeps over her.

Blackout. In the darkness, a scream.

A spotlight on the artwork:

John R. Goodman

"Good times — Good friends — Good food"

THROWN FROM A TRAIN

When Karen's daughter, Jewel, is taken by "Dirty Harry", Karen fears the worst. But Harry has been nursing a secret, and there are bad things even beyond Karen's imagination.

Characters

KAREN — *A single mother*

HARRY — *A reclusive elderly man*

JEWEL — *Karen's daughter, about 13*

Lights up. Karen sits on a chair DSC on an otherwise empty stage. She seems to be addressing someone in the audience.

KAREN. Is he dead?

She appears to listen to a brief reply.

But soon, yeah?

She nods.

Is he in agony? Like really, really bad pain? Let's hope so, eh? I want to think of him in writhing in agony, crying out for his Mummy - but she'll have been dead for ages, right? So he can be with her. In hell I mean. Being poked with red hot pokers for ever and ever. Right up his arse. Watching his old mother being poked up her arse too. But let him die slowly first. Get a few shit hospital meals and think about what he done. What he done to my little Jewel. Some people don't fuckin' deserve to live, I know that.

She nods again, emphatically.

I'm not thick, you know. Don't go thinking I'm stupid. I know I'm going to prison. Should be all right - they all hate paedos, don't they? I'll be a hero. Kid's'll be OK I reckon. I'm a crap mother anyway. Jewel's more

> of a mum than I'll ever be. I can see that. I'm not that thick. Yeah, I know I said I didn't do it but I knew I couldn't get away with it even when I was saying it. It's instinct, innit. He just goes - that first policeman, the cute one - he goes, "What happened here" and I go, "He opened the door and he tripped. He fell, he fell on the knife." And he looks at him and he looks at me and we're both all covered in it and his mate's on the radio for an ambulance and he goes, "How many bloody times did he fall on the knife?"

She snorts.

> You've got to laugh. There'll be no blokes where I'm going. I won't mind. They do your head in anyway. It was all for the babies. But the babies were never like my Jewel. I'll remember her every day. What it was like, with her.

Blackout. Karen exits.

Pause, then shouting from off stage:

JEWEL. We could eat proper if you didn't drink it all. Where you going now? No, don't bother, I know where. Who with? Steve? Rashid? Gaz? That twat with the lazy eye? Or is it somebody new tonight? You're a slag and

I hate you.

KAREN. Jewel, I'm your mother - you can't talk to me like that.

Lights up. Jewel runs on stage.

JEWEL. Just did, slag.

She puts on some cherry red lipstick, quickly and sloppily. Karen appears on stage

KAREN. Give me my lipstick you thieving little whore.

Jewel dodges away.

JEWEL. Takes one to know one, slag.

KAREN. Don't call me slag, you gobby little bitch.

She snatches the lipstick.

JEWEL. Oh I'm sorry, "Karen".

KAREN. I told you, you can call me Mum when we're on our own.

JEWEL. Look, they all know you're a mum, Mum. Stop pretending like I'm your sister or a neighbour or

> whatever. What time tonight?

KAREN. Depends. Ten. Half eleven if someone's buying. Do your homework.

JEWEL. Done it. He never marks it anyway.

KAREN. Yeah, I don't know why you bother.

JEWEL. Might go next door to Lorraine for a bit.

KAREN. Well don't leave 'em on their own too long. What? Don't look at me like that.

JEWEL. They'll be all right for half an hour. They've got the Nintendo. And my mobile.

KAREN. Well wipe that mess off your kisser if you go out. And just be here when I get back, that's all.

Karen kisses Jewel on the cheek and exits. Jewel looks after her then smiles affectionately.

JEWEL. Slag.

Blackout. Pause, then a scream from offstage. The scream is muffled and the sound of a struggle approaches the stage. There is a ripping noise. In the dim light we vaguely see a figure bundle another figure into the chair. As the lights slowly fade up we see the ripping noise comes from a roll of gaffer tape with which Harry is securing Jewel into the chair. She is already gagged, with her wrists bound by the tape. Harry is breathless from the effort. He goes off stage and returns with another chair which he places opposite Jewel and collapses into it.

HARRY. I'm sorry. I'm sorry. I'm so sorry.

Harry repeats this until he has his breath back. Jewel struggles.

HARRY. I'm not going to hurt you. That's a promise. I know how you must feel and you won't want to believe me, but I'm not going to hurt you. I'm going to let you go but I have to tell you something first. And give you something. Do you understand?

Jewel makes angry muffled noises through the gag. She responds in the same way throughout the following.

HARRY. I'm sorry, I'm sorry. I tried to talk to you before but you wouldn't listen. I know, I know, it was the same for me. No, no. To me, he was frightening, foreign. You weren't frightened. To you, I was just… irrelevant. Do you know what that means? Some neighbour to be ignored. Some sad old man who had nothing to do with your life. Yes, I see you understand. Well, you can ignore me afterwards I suppose. I hadn't really thought about afterwards.

Pause.

HARRY. There was this man up the street from me, when I was about your age, and he spoke with a strange accent. He'd come from Poland or somewhere during the war and could not go back. Have they told you about the war? The Second World War?

Jewel nods.

HARRY. We thought he was a bit... strange. He'd give us sweets - liquorice comfits and so on — and he'd ask us about school, but grown-ups didn't like him and told us to stay away from him. He seemed to like me but he had big bushy eyebrows like caterpillars that made me nervous. I was a bit... revulsed. The more he tried to single me out, the more I'd try to avoid him. I'd go the long way round to get home. Are you getting this?

Jewel nods then tries to speak through the gag.

HARRY. Sorry. I'll take it off in a moment but you have to promise not to shout and scream. OK? Anyway, one day — it was foggy, like it never seems to be these days — he grabbed me. Stuffed a scarf in my mouth, bent my arm behind my back and took me back to his flat. Tied me up with washing line

Jewel makes agitated noises.

HARRY. In a moment. Sorry, sorry. I was terrified. You seem to be a lot braver than I was. I hoped you would be. I couldn't do this with a screamer. Funny, for years I wondered why he picked me — why didn't he choose a girl? And today, today I understand. It's more complicated with a girl. But there'll be no funny stuff, promise. I'm really not going to hurt you, you know. I'm too old for all that now, anyway. Will you be quiet if I take that off?

Pause. She nods, slowly. He undoes the gag, with some difficulty. He gets out a knife and unpicks the knot. When the gag comes off she takes a huge breath. He gestures for silence with one hand, holds the knife away with the other.

JEWEL. So, it's Harry isn't it? You must know what they say about you. "Dirty Harry". Always hanging around opposite school. Why did you choose me?

HARRY. When I first saw you — you were younger — I thought you must be like her — the girl on the train. I don't know why. I have no idea what she looked like.

But I've imagined. Dreamed. Then I saw what you were like with the younger kids. Not just your brothers and sisters, all of them. They like you. You seem to care. And I just got more and more certain — you were the one.

JEWEL. You're not right in the head. You know that don't you?

HARRY. Yes... yes, I know that. How could I be with this hanging over me? I thought I wouldn't do it. Then I thought I had to do it. Then I thought I couldn't do it. Then I was old and I thought "Time's running out". Time's running out.

He fishes in his jacket pocket and brings out a dog-eared postcard in a clear plastic bag. The card is covered on both sides with faint, tiny handwriting in pencil.

HARRY. He didn't hurt me, he let me go, just like I'll let you go. But first, he told me how he got this. He was younger and walking through the countryside. He told me where but I couldn't get all those unpronounceable names. He was trying to run away, to join some freedom fighters. He wasn't much more than a kid himself but he wanted to fight the Germans who had marched into his country. When he saw the railway tracks he thought they'd lead the way, so he walked alongside them. Then, when he saw the train coming he thought he might be able to ride it, like some American hobo. It was a freight train and moving quite slowly. He hid behind a bush so the driver would not see him and he was going to try and run and climb up between the trucks when the engine was past him. But then he saw the German soldiers on the footplate. They had guns. The train rattled past. It smelt terrible, he said. The trucks were all chained and barred. He saw a little hand come out of a grill near the top of one truck and throw something white. It fluttered to the ground and when the train was gone he picked it up. He kept it all his life until he grabbed me and made me take it. He told me, "Keep it. Remember it. And when you are a man, give it to a child." Then he let me go.

JEWEL. So that's it? You're gonna give me that, then I can go?

HARRY. Will you remember? For the rest of your life?

JEWEL. 'Spose. Not much happens 'round here. I'll call the police if no-one's done it already. Then I'll remember 'cos it'll be in the papers.

HARRY. I suppose you can read?

Thrown from a Train

JEWEL. 'Course I can read. Don't disrespect me.

HARRY. No. I'll try not to. Sorry. Read this. Aloud. I'll hold it.

JEWEL. Why should I, pervert?

Harry sighs, gestures towards the gag with the knife.

JEWEL. It wants to be closer. That writing's tiny.

Harry moves behind her and holds the card in front of her. Her face changes and she reads in the voice of Anna, the card's author.

JEWEL. Dearest Papa, We send all our kisses to you, Mama and Toivi and me. You see I write in English like you teach me. Perhaps they do not read English, these Germans. You see I remember to be careful, like you say. It is hot on this train and there are no seats. So many are standing that we hold each other up. We take it in turns to sit or lie down but the floor is very dirty and the wagon smells. I think animals were here before. The train stops often for no reason. It is stopped now so I am able to write. An old lady gave the little pencil. She says I may keep it even though it has a silver knob and a little silk tassel. We are being resettled in the East — they say somewhere in Ukraine. We have had two nights on the train. I think

> the old lady's husband is dead but Mama says he is very sick and sleeps the whole time. Children are sitting on him and he does not move. The old lady just smiles at them but at night I hear her cry. A lot of people cry but I try to be brave for Toivi. Mama cries too when she thinks we are asleep. Oh! We are moving again.

Pause. Jewel bows her head. Harry rotates the card and points to more writing.

> It's another day now and the train is stopped again. The old lady died in the night and guards came and threw her and her husband off the train. Others too but it did not seem to make more space. I am very thirsty and can only whisper. Mama hums to Toivi but he is very quiet. She says we are with you now in your prison. We are a family again. I'm trying to think of our old room above the shop, playing with the dreidel at Hannukah. No room. No room on this card. So many people here and so alone.

Harry twists the card to another angle.

> Papa, I miss your whiskers and tickles. I will see you again, in a kinder time.

Your loving daughter,

Anna.

Pause. Harry sobs.

JEWEL. What's that all about then?

HARRY. There was no address, no last name, nowhere he could send the card. He waited for the kinder time, but it came too late. The train wasn't going to the Ukraine, you see. It was going to a place called Treblinka. Anna and Toivi — her brother I suppose — and their mother were not being "resettled". When they arrived, it looked just like a real station, with a clock. The clock was just painted wood. There was a room where they could leave their luggage. The women and children were separated from the men. They had to be deloused after the journey. They took off all their clothes for the communal showers. They must have been shy — embarrassed — fearful. Women and girls wept as their hair was cut off and their heads were shaved. Perhaps Anna had very long hair she was very proud of. I don't know why they needed the hair, but none of this makes sense, so why not? In the shower room they waited for the water to come but what they got was Zyklon B, a cyanide-based pesticide developed by a Nobel Prize-winning

> Jew. They all died within 20 minutes, some quickly, some screaming. Many bodies were recovered hunched up, skin all pink with coloured spots, bleeding from the ears and nose, foaming at the mouth.

Harry shakes Jewel by the shoulders.

HARRY. Do you see? Do you see?

Jewel nods, slowly. For the first time, she seems frightened

JEWEL. I see. You had to do it. Let me go now. It will be all right.

There is a savage pounding on the door.

KAREN [*off*]. Open this door you dirty old git! I know you've got her in there. You'd better not have done nothin' to her!

More banging on the door. Harry takes the kitchen knife and cuts the tape holding Jewel's wrists.

KAREN. Open this door you perv! I've called the police. You're up Shit Street.

Harry gives Jewel the postcard. She looks at him. The hammering on the door stops.

HARRY. Take it. Keep it. Remember it. Then, when you are
      old, give it to a child.

Karen starts up again. With the knife still in his hand, Harry goes to the door. Karen is still hammering and calling abuse. We hear the door open and Karen's shriek of rage.

Blackout. Silence.

Printed in Great Britain
by Amazon